W9-BDY-000

BIBLIO VAMPIRO

A Vampire Handbook

First edition for North America published in 2010 by
Barron's Educational Series, Inc.

Copyright © 2010 Marshall Editions

All rights reserved. No part of this book may be
reproduced or distributed in any form or by any means
without the written permission of the copyright owner.

All inquiries should be addressed to:
Barron's Educational Series, Inc.
250 Wireless Boulevard
Hauppauge, NY 11788
www.barronseduc.com

ISBN-13: 978-0-7641-6341-8
ISBN-10: 0-7641-6341-8
Library of Congress Control Number:
2010920896

M VAIH

Conceived, designed, and produced by
Marshall Editions
The Old Brewery
6 Blundell Street
London N7 9BH
www.marshalleditions.com

Commissioning Editor: Laura Price
Art Director: Ivo Marloh
Design: The Bookmakers
Picture Manager: Veneta Bullen
Production: Nikki Ingram

Date of manufacture: August 2010
Manufactured by: 1010 Printing International Ltd.
Color separation by: Modern Age Repro House Ltd.,
    Hong Kong

Printed in China

9 8 7 6 5 4 3 2

BIBLIO VAMPIRO

A Vampire Handbook

Dr. Robert Curran

BARRON'S

What is a Vampire?

What do you know about vampires? You will undoubtedly have questions. These creatures conjure up various images and thoughts — mostly scary ones.

Vampires are creatures from mythology and folklore. Vampire stories and beliefs have been captured in popular culture or passed on through generations by word of mouth. While people really have been accused of drinking blood and being vampires, we do not know for sure whether vampires are real or not.

Are vampires human?

This is a difficult question to answer, but vampires are usually human corpses. They can take many forms, have different abilities, and come in many "types" (*see pages 20-35*), but almost all were once living people.

Above *Vampires prefer to feed on human blood which, while messy, is a good clue when vampire spotting.*
Right *Can you spot why this isn't a true vampire? See how his fingers cast a shadow on the wall. A true vampire would never cast a shadow like this.*

DO THEY REALLY DRINK BLOOD?

Many do, yes. They feed on the blood of humans or animals, and from this they gain energy and the ability to live forever. Others take life force or energy from humans, which has the same immortalizing effect.

WHAT POWERS DO THEY HAVE?

This is another difficult question, mainly because each vampire is different. Vampires can take the form of animals such as dogs and, perhaps most famously, bats. Some vampires can fly. Others are known for their strength, both mental and physical, and are often said to have supernatural powers.

Some can transform themselves into a misty nothingness — ideal in times of escape or entry. They have heightened senses — they can smell and hear you from afar — and some have been known to communicate silently through telepathy.

Vampires are immortal and do not age from the time they become vampires, as long as they feed regularly on blood. This immortality also gives them the power to heal themselves and, in very unusual circumstances, others.

If this has whetted your appetite for more, please read on…

ABOVE *Vampires taking the form of bats to feed on a sleeping human. Who knows why she's not in bed.*
LEFT *The undead rising from their coffins for a night of feeding, caught by a passerby — maybe not so lucky for him.*

What Do They Look Like?

What does a vampire look like? Do they look the same as you or me? In many cases they do, and this makes them difficult to detect. However, there are some differences...

Look closely at the color of their skin or their eyes. The skin will usually be extremely pale and the eyes will have a reddish tinge about them, suggesting that they may not be quite human. They will also be extremely thin – this can sometimes make them appear very elegant – due to the fact that they do not eat normal food but subsist mainly on blood.

Vampires also do not appear to age in the way that we do but often seem reasonably youthful. However,

FAR LEFT *A classic Strigoii vampire, human in form but with monstrous staring eyes and deathly pale skin (see page 20).*
LEFT *A vampire concealing itself in a mist. This is an invaluable skill in times of danger or when stalking prey.*
BELOW *A Malaysian Penanggal vampire. This one has clearly fed as the head has rejoined the body (see page 22).*

shape of dragons or lizards that do not necessarily drink blood. In Mexico and South America, they can appear as no more than balls of light, which draw off energy from sleeping people. In Japan, they can appear as drifting spirits with no feet or sometimes as enormous spider-like creatures with many eyes. In most cases, such creatures only appear at night – though some do appear during the daytime – which may be another clue as to their true nature.

if deprived of blood for long periods of time, the vampire body will start to decay and become a rotting corpse, just as it would be in the tomb. In parts of Denmark and Norway, for instance, their skin may be black with bits of rotting bone showing through, or terribly white, as if just risen from the grave.

Descriptions of vampires are a bit more complicated in some parts of the world because they do not even appear human. For example, in some places like China or the Philippines, they can take on the

WHERE DO THEY LIVE?

Some people believe that vampires are only found in Eastern Europe, in places steeped in vampire mystery such as Transylvania, but this is not altogether true.

Although they *are* found in the folklore of such places, vampires really exist all over the world. They may appear different and may even absorb human energy in different ways, but they are all essentially vampires.

They exist in Norway and in the Philippines, in Ireland, and in Malaysia. Some live in remote mountains, and others live deep in steaming jungles. Perhaps one of the reasons why many people think that

they come from Romania, and why some of the early films about them were set there, is because at one time there were numerous stories about them in that part of the world.

Vampires also don't necessarily tend to live in ruined castles or crypts as many stories suggest; given the proper conditions and precautions, there is no reason why a

ABOVE *Vampires love coffins. In Eastern Europe, vampires often sleep in coffins, probably because there is little chance they will be disturbed.*

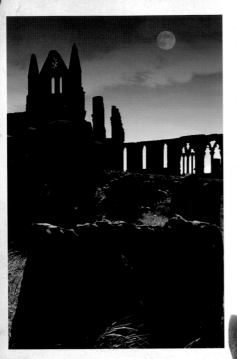

vampire couldn't live in an ordinary house. There may even be one existing somewhere near you.

Many vampires do stay well away from humans, hiding away in remote tombs, mausoleums, and cemeteries where they can exist untouched – most of them want as little contact with humans as possible, except for nourishment. However, there may also be some in our bustling towns and cities. Take a closer look at your neighbors, if you dare!

LEFT *Old castles and creepy ruins used to be popular among vampires, but now they're just as likely to be living in town.* BELOW *The steamy jungles of the Philippines are home to the dragon-like Aswang vampires (see page 24).*

10 Vital Ways to Spot a Vampire

Detecting a vampire is not always easy, especially when they sometimes bear a close resemblance to the living. However, there are a few tell-tale clues:

1 Vampires that retain human form have extremely pale skin, while others resemble flames, dragons, floating heads, or even trolls.

2 Vampires may have a particular aversion to garlic, especially large, raw cloves. They also dislike the smell of onions frying.

3 Silver will repel some vampires, while iron repels others. The metal burns their skin and repels their image, which is why they cannot be photographed.

4 Vampires avoid sunlight, as it burns their skin much more quickly than it burns yours.

5 Vampires fear holy ground, churches, and holy symbols such as crucifixes. Most will turn away from a cross.

6 Vampires cast no shadows, even in the strongest light.

7 Vampires stick to the shadows whenever they can to keep out of sight and hunt their prey.

8 Vampires avoid mirrors, as they have no reflection. Some say this is because they have no soul; others say that the silver backing on mirrors repels the vampire's image.

9 Romanian vampires may be extremely obsessive and spend hours gathering small stones.

10 All vampires have been known to sleep in coffins or in crypts, and many make their homes in cemeteries.

Right *If you really want to spot a vampire, spooky nighttime graveyards are ideal. Recently awoken from a day's rest, the graveyard vampires will be up and ready for action.*

How to Avoid a Vampire (very important)

Where you are, where you live, and the type of vampire that you wish to avoid will all affect what you do if you are confronted by one.

W herever people practice the Christian faith, it may be that some Christian symbols will protect you from vampire attack. Some vampires are driven away by a cross or crucifix, or by holy water, which burns vampire skin like scalding liquid.

Silver can repel some vampires, and sunlight is effective against many types — if you can get them to leave the dark! This is usually tricky because they're either asleep during the day, or determined to keep out of the light.

In parts of Romania (*see map on page 75*) you can throw poppy seeds around if a vampire attacks. Local vampires are compulsive creatures and many will stop to pick up the seeds, giving you time to escape.

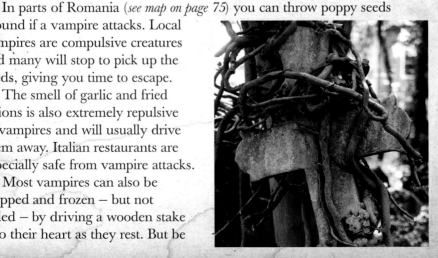

The smell of garlic and fried onions is also extremely repulsive to vampires and will usually drive them away. Italian restaurants are especially safe from vampire attacks.

Most vampires can also be stopped and frozen — but not killed — by driving a wooden stake into their heart as they rest. But be careful! Make sure that the wood you use is suitable for the vampire that you are trying to suspend — for instance, you will need oak wood in Russia, yew in Serbia, and rowan in Scotland. If the wood is not the right kind, it will have no effect and the vampire will certainly attack you for having plunged a piece of wood into its chest.

If you are trying to avoid the *tikoloshe* vampire (*see page 26*) of South Africa, then it is advisable to sleep on a bed, propped up on stacks of bricks. This will stop the vampire from climbing up and attacking you.

To avoid the attentions of a *dybukk* — a Jewish vampire — sleep with a protective iron charm and tie red ribbons around your bed.

The only sure way of getting rid of a vampire for good, however, is to cut off its head and burn the rest of its body, which is not very pleasant.

Left *Religious artifacts, such as crosses and holy water, may deter a vampire attack.*
Right *A vampire being vanquished — probably the only way to make sure he doesn't attack anyone again. Don't try this at home.*

The Three Golden Rules

What should you do if you see a vampire? Well, avoidance is the best form of defense, so try to stay away from places that are connected to the vampire kind.

If you should happen to run into a vampire by accident, what should you do? There are three golden rules you should follow, so listen carefully. Here are the rules that should keep you safe.

Protection

You should have some sort of protection with you. This may include a crucifix, which may hold the vampire back for some time, or holy water or silver, which may severely burn its skin, or some sort of iron talisman. These will probably give you time to make your escape. **Note**: Such protections may or may not work, and even if they do, they are only protective for a short time.

Distraction

Have a pocketful of grain to scatter before the vampire attacks. Because vampires are rather tidy creatures, they will attempt to clear up the spilled grain before attacking you. In some cases, however, this may only work for a moment or so before the vampire realizes what you are doing, so have your escape plan ready.

Diversion

Try to make sure that there is fresh or running water – for example, a river or a stream – as a barrier between you and the vampire. It is well known that no unholy thing can cross running water, so as long as you stay on the other side, the vampire cannot get to you. You are then free to make your escape.

Although these rules are useful, you should note that because vampires in various parts of the world differ greatly, the above rules may not always work. They have also been drawn up to deal with largely European vampires; Eastern vampires may be very different and require quite different protections. But the best advice is to keep away from places where you think vampires might be!

ABOVE *A standard vampire hunter's kit, which includes holy water, a crucifix, and a small pistol (perhaps loaded with silver). While useful, it depends on the vampire if any of this will work.*

Types of Vampires

From the terrible Aswang dragons of the Philippines to the classic Strigoii of Romania, it's vital that you can tell your vampires apart if you are to have any hope of surviving a meeting with one.

STRIGOII VAMPIRES

[**stree**-goy **vam**-pyrs]

The Strigoii, the vampires of Romania, are often what we imagine the Undead to be like. Virtually indistinguishable from the living, they lurk close to us, thinking up ways in which to harm the human world.

Generally, the returning Romanian dead fall into two categories – the *Moroii* – or the blessed dead who are good – and the *Strigoii* – who are infinitely evil. In many respects, these dead, when they rise from the grave, carry on pretty much as they have done in life. The Strigoii, therefore, were unpopular, spiteful, dangerous, or downright mean when alive, and continue to be so after death.

GOLDEN RULES FOR STRIGOII

1 Try to avoid them whenever possible.
2 Scatter small items such as pebbles or poppy seeds. They should stop to collect them.
3 Carry a bulb of wild garlic or a religious artifact – this may repel them.
4 Head for a stream; they cannot cross fresh or running water.
5 Some cannot enter a house without invitation, so be careful who you invite home.

Unless one knows that this is a dead person, it is sometimes difficult to tell them from the living, but there are telltale signs. They do not speak but have a "watchfulness" about them, and are aware of what is going on around them. It may seem as if they know what you are thinking or that they know what will happen next. This is probably due to their heightened senses.

Although most of them walk at night, you may see them during the day, yet they are pretty easy to spot if you are aware. Check them out in bright sunlight. You'll know if you're with a Strigoii, as they cast no shadow, even in the strongest light. Similarly, they have no reflection in a mirror, so if you're on the lookout for vampires it might be a good idea to carry one.

and all of them hate garlic – either wild or in cooking – but then again, so do some humans. Finally, they don't like Christian symbols, but you shouldn't completely depend on it.

In some parts of Romania they eat nothing at all

BELOW *Look out for the high, pointy collar and the big, black cape. Of course, the Strigoii don't dress like this any more.*

PENANGGAL VAMPIRES

[pen-an-**gaal vam**-pyrs]

Perhaps the most terrifying of all vampires is the Malaysian Penanggal. In some parts of the East, it is believed that these vampires can detach parts of their bodies and send them out to drain the life force from the living.

The Penanggal or Penanggalan is one of the most common forms of the Undead to be found in Malaysia. It is usually no more than the floating head of a woman with a blood-ringed mouth – these vampires are always female – trailing her intestines after her. The Penanggal is usually controlled by a dark spirit or evil sorcerer.

Malaysian vampires travel mainly at night, flying through the air. They have incredibly sharp teeth and staring eyes, with which they can see quite clearly in the dark. Sometimes they emit a dreadful shriek and attack mainly young children or pregnant women. In fact, the Penanggal was a mother herself at one time but died in childbirth, and this has turned her into the horrifying being.

When the Penanggal has eaten, it returns to its tomb where the head joins with the rest of the body. If attacked, the creature can shoot fire through its nostrils to burn any assailant.

GOLDEN RULES FOR PENANGGAL

1 Try to lure the creature into a bush where its entrails will be caught and it will be largely helpless.
2 Alternatively, lure it into a container and trap it. However, be warned, it might turn to smoke and escape.
3 Be sure to block your ears to protect yourself from its deafening shriek.
4 If intent on destroying the Penanggal, try to find its grave and destroy the rest of its body by fire. This, however, is extremely dangerous.

Below *The bodiless, floating head of the terrifying Penanggal hunts for its nightly feed.*

Aswang Vampires

[**az**-wang **vam**-pyrs]

Of all the Undead, the Aswang of the Philippines certainly does not resemble any vampire that we might recognize. In fact, it is not even human in shape.

Right *A rare image of the dreaded Aswang at rest. Scaly, winged, and dragon-like, this evil hunter terrorizes the Philippines.*

ABOVE *A fleeting vision of an Aswang in flight – probably on its way to feed.*

GOLDEN RULES FOR ASWANG

1 Sleep with a bag of salt mixed with human urine around your neck. Both are powerfully protective.
2 Make sure there are no flies in your room; they might be Aswangs in another guise.
3 Look out for hollow tongues poking out of your ceiling!

More than anything, the Aswang resembles a small, scaly dragon with bat-like wings and a large snout, which contains a long and hollow tongue.

In the lore of some Filipino islands, the Aswang is not the soul of a dead person at all but the corrupted spirit of one who has never really been born. Others believe that they are living sorcerers who can change their shape at will and who exist only to do harm to their neighbors.

Aswang are most commonly female and generally attack sleeping males. Their favorite prey is small children, but they will also attack the old and feeble who can't protect themselves.

Usually, an Aswang will land on the roof of a house while the people inside are asleep and hide along the gutter until all is quiet. Then, from its snout, a long tongue emerges, which it lowers into the room where the sleeper is lying. The tip of the tongue is incredibly sharp but the tongue itself is hollow, and through it the vampire sucks up either blood or sweat – it can feed on both. As it feeds, the Aswang swells and its chest grows to an enormous size.

There are many types of Aswang, depending on which Philippine island you are on. Some islanders believe that the upper and lower parts of the body can split and perform evil deeds separately from each other. Others believe that the creature takes the form of a tik-tik, a small, owl-like bird that drinks through a curved beak.

TIKOLOSHE VAMPIRES

[**ti**-ko-low-**she vam**-pyrs]

Is a vampire actually the spirit of a dead person, or can it also be some sort of demon? Or is it really a spirit that is controlled by witchcraft?

This is what we have to think about when we consider the *tikoloshe* or *tikoloshie*, a South African vampire that appears in the lore of a number of tribes there. For some tribes it is the shrunken body of someone who has been harmed by witches. If a sorcerer can obtain a piece of the victim's excrement, he or she can draw the life from them and make them a tiny, withered husk.

On the African Gold Coast, however, the tikoloshe is the name of a vampire wizard who has hooks at the end of its legs instead of feet and who drinks blood to sustain itself. The main description of the tikoloshe comes from the Xhosa people of southern Lesotho, who say that it is a small, monkey-like creature that sometimes takes the form of a great black bird with a human skull for a head. This type of vampire does not always drink blood – though it can – but sometimes draws off the energy through the skin of a sleeper in the same way that energy vampires do (*see page 34*).

GOLDEN RULES FOR TIKOLOSHE

1 Make sure that your bed is well above the ground so the tikoloshe cannot climb up.
2 Draw a circle on the ground and sprinkle it with magic herbal powder. The tikoloshe will not be able to cross it.
3 Tikoloshe often live in caves along riverbanks, so avoid these if you can.
4 Look for dark, slitted eyes with no pupils.

The tikoloshe is a great shape-changer and it approaches its victims – who are usually female – in the guise of a handsome man, offering to carry bundles of sticks or heavy clothes for her. When it is alone, it will revert to its real shape and attack. It will also attack people as they are sleeping – particularly the very young or the old who cannot defend themselves.

Below *A dancer in a tikoloshe mask. Some believe that wearing the mask of the tikoloshe and performing a ritual dance will keep the vampire away. Let's hope it's true.*

SAMPIRO VAMPIRES

[sam-**pyr**-o **vam**-pyrs]

Sampiro are rather bizarre-looking Albanian vampires who initially only attack their own families or communities. This is not to say they aren't extremely dangerous and will attack and drink the blood of anyone who crosses their path.

S ampiro exist in remote mountain areas such as the Bosnian Alps. Originally, they were believed to be the corpses of Moslem Turks who had died among Christians, but later the belief widened to include anybody who had not been properly buried. Those in danger of becoming Sampiro include those with Turkish backgrounds and those who have not been buried with the proper ceremony of the Albanian Orthodox Church.

In these instances, about 3–4 hours after being buried, the Sampiro will rise and prowl around, still wrapped in its burial winding sheet. Strangely, however, they will now be wearing large high heels on which they totter unsteadily along. Its eyes are as big as car headlights, and as it moves it makes "kissing noises" to draw its prey. It will first attack its own family but will then venture out into the wider community, falling upon those whom it encounters.

LEFT *Bosnian sampiro vampires are unusually tall (thanks to their odd passion for high heels) and clearly no longer human. If you spot one... run!*

There is no known way to destroy a Sampiro apart from ensuring that corpses are buried properly. In Northern Albania, however, it is believed that if a wolf attacks a Sampiro — it is sometimes known as a Lugat in the Northern Provinces — it will bite the vampire's legs off. The Sampiro will then return to its tomb forever.

Note: If the Sampiro remains undetected for 30 years, it does not have to return to its tomb but can remain in the living world forever as long as it keeps to the shadows and cool areas. It is then known as a *kukuthi*.

GOLDEN RULES FOR SAMPIRO

1 Walk quickly — the Sampiro is always unsteady on its high heels and cannot move too fast.
2 Ensure that you have attended an Orthodox service at least one hour before any meeting — a Roman Catholic service will not do.
3 Ensure that you have nothing around you that suggests the Moslem religion or Turkish nationality — these are the particular targets of the Sampiro.
4 To spot one, look out for anyone who is taller than most humans and wrapped in a grave cloth or winding sheet.

VRYKOKOLAS VAMPIRES

[**vree**-ko-ko-lass **vam**-pyrs]

Vrykokolas are Greek vampires, which are also known as kathakanes in parts of the country such as the island of Crete.

Almost indistinguishable from living people – although there are certain signs – vrykokolas have the advantage of being able to walk in broad daylight, usually appearing around noon.

Despite being similar to normal living humans, the vrykokolas have a reddish tinge to their hair, which is unusual among Greeks. They have a lost and vacant stare about them, cast no shadow in either sunlight or lamplight, and seldom speak.

They do not necessarily drink blood, though they can do so if they wish, but can cause great harm to the living. They are violent and will often steal foodstuffs such as corn and beans and wine that has been left out for

RIGHT *Easily mixing with the living, only slight reddish tints to the hair and sometimes eyes allow you to spot a vrykokola vampire. Can you spot one here?*

the next day's meal. They often drag the bedclothes from sleepers and beat them severely. Their voices are sometimes heard, mocking people on their way to Church.

There are various ways of becoming a vrykokola, including dying without the proper rites of the Church; being conceived or born on a Holy Day, which is considered a great blasphemy; having an animal pass over or below the corpse before burial; dying from a plague or unknown disease; and, finally, having lived an unpleasant life.

GOLDEN RULES FOR VRYKOKOLAS

1. Avoidance is always best.
2. If a vrykokola is suspected, ask a bishop to have the tomb opened and an exorcism performed. An ordinary priest will be of no use.
3. Scatter either meal or beans. The vrykokola will stop to eat these, giving you time to escape.
4. Call forth the name of an angel, at which point the vrykokola will disappear.
5. They often stay close to cesspools and trash to which they are drawn.

DRAUGR VAMPIRES

[**drow**-ger **vam**-pyrs]

From the land of trolls and giants come the Scandinavian vampires — the Draugr. Hoarders of Viking treasures, these fearsome creatures attack anyone they think might steal their gold – and that means everyone.

Having set up their stinking nests near the graves of Viking warriors – some of which were full of ancient treasure that the draugr claim as their own – the draugr sit and count their gold until nightfall, when they roam the Earth in search of human prey.

GOLDEN RULES FOR DRAUGR

1 Avoidance is the first and most important rule.
2 Do not attempt garlic or crucifixes; they just won't work.
3 Draugr prowl by night and sleep by day.
4 They may be able to change size at will, so never turn your back on one.
5 Some draugr are immune to weapons so it's best to have a backup plan.

Superhuman in strength and always looking for a fight, the draugr are possibly the nastiest of the nightwalkers. Perhaps it is their love of treasure that causes the draugr to attack the living, as they believe their secret hoards are under threat from thieves. Or perhaps they are simply the meanest bunch of bloodsuckers around. It is unlikely that we'll ever know for sure, as few who meet them live to tell the tale.

You certainly could never mistake a draugr for a human, so they are easy to spot. Their skin is either pitch black or deathly white, and they are surrounded at all times by

a terrible smell – the stench of death and despair.

Only humans with great courage and determination could hope to overcome the draugr – and even those heroes would have to go to great lengths to secure victory. Some draugr are immune to weapons; others can change size at will. Such is their power that, once dead, a draugr's body must be destroyed to stop it from coming back.

ABOVE *The skull of a draugr possesses many hidden dangers for unwary travelers, especially thieves.*

ENERGY VAMPIRES

[en-er-**gee vam**-pyrs]

Not all vampires appear as humanoids. Energy (sometimes known as "psychic") vampires can appear as no more than small balls of light but, of course, this makes them no less dangerous.

These vampires are perhaps most closely associated with witchcraft and are often said to be the malignant spirits of dead witches. They are found in South and Central America and parts of Asia, and often appear as globes of light that float above graveyards and travel at incredible speeds across the country.

GOLDEN RULES FOR ENERGY VAMPIRES

1 Avoidance is the only real precaution, if at all possible.
2 If not, douse the vampire's gravesite in holy water.

nearby. The most famous of these vampires existed in the form of a discolored, human-shaped piece of earth in the cellar of 135 Benefit Street, Providence, Rhode Island. Until it was eventually destroyed, this vampire was able to draw the energies from those who lived in the house above, causing continual sickness. The tale formed the basis of a story by American writer H.P. Lovecraft – *The Shunned House.*

In parts of Mexico, small flames – some no bigger than a candle flame – hover outside the windows of houses, drawing out the energy of anyone inside.

There is actually little that can be done about them, except to seek out the actual gravesite of the witch or sorcerer and either douse it in holy water or acid, or burn the body within. This will hopefully stop the activities of the energy vampire but once again, as so often, such things are not certain.

They do not feast on the *blood* of humans, but rather draw off *energy* from their victims, leaving them weak and listless.

They can also appear as patches of mold or fungus that do not move but can absorb energies from those

ABOVE *These flaming vampires can move at great speed and, although they will not drink your blood, your very lifeforce is at stake!*

VAMPIRE TALES

From the deadly ladies of Rhode Island to the bloodthirsty desires of Romanian countesses, these true tales of vampire horror have become legends in their own countries, and chilling warnings to us all.

THE OLDEST VAMPIRE

ABHARTACH

Probably the oldest written vampire story in the world comes from the North of Ireland and deals not with an Undead Romanian count, but with a barbaric and bloodthirsty Irish chieftain. In Ireland, vampires are known as neamh-marbh (walking dead), or dearg-dul (red drinkers), and the chieftain in question seems to have been the worst of them all.

In the fifth and sixth centuries, large parts of Ireland were divided into small kingdoms, some not very large but each ruled over by its own "king" (no more than a local warlord). The present-day area of Glenullin near the town of Garvagh in North Derry was, at this time, a patchwork of such kingdoms, one of which was ruled by a chieftain called Abhartach. Little is known about him but it's thought that he was a dwarf, that he was deformed, and that he was a powerful magician. He was also cruel and greatly feared by his subjects. However, none of them had the courage to kill him, so they hired another chieftain named Cahan, from across the mountains, to come and slay him for them. Cahan came and challenged Abhartach to a battle and after a mighty fight, slew the evil Abhartach, burying him standing up in his grave, which suited an Irish chieftain.

Aʙᴏᴠᴇ *A suspended vampire, staked and buried, may appear mummified as the lifeforce that allows it to rise from the dead is kept at bay.*

However, the next day, Abhartach was back among his people and his behavior was worse than ever; he demanded a bowlful of blood taken from the crook of their arms as a tribute, and drank their blood freely.

Cahan came again, and once again slew Abhartach in battle, burying him as before. But nonetheless the corpse returned, just as evil as before and demanding the same gory tribute of the blood of his people.

Baffled, Cahan went to a local holy man who lived in nearby Gortnamoyah Forest to ask for advice on what was happening and his help in this strange event.

"He is not actually dead," the holy man told him after much contemplation, "but is kept alive by his magic arts. He is one of the *neamh-marbh*, the night-walking dead. He cannot be killed but he can be suspended. Strike him with a sword of yew wood, bury him upside down, scatter thorns around his grave, and place a great stone or monument over his grave to keep him in it. Only then will he give you peace."

So all of this Cahan did, killing Abhartach for a third time and erecting a great leacht or sepulchre over the grave where he lay buried upside down. From then on the area became known as Slaghtaverty (Abhartach's leacht), a name which it still bears today. The stones of the gravesite are now scattered, but a huge capstone lies across the grave. A small tree, which is supposed to have grown from the thorns that Cahan scattered, still flourishes there. Even so, few local people will approach the site after dark. They still speak of the "grave of the man who was buried three times," and it is said that if the capstone is actually raised Abhartach will be free to rise again to prowl the area.

The story of Abhartach was once well known all across Ireland and appears as history in some early books, such as Dr. Geoffrey Keating's *A General History of Ireland*, published between 1629 and 1631, making it one of the oldest recorded vampire tales. It has even been suggested that this story was known to Bram Stoker and may have partly inspired his great vampire novel *Dracula*. Even if this isn't true, there is little doubt that there is a vampire lying beneath the quiet Irish landscape, ready to rise at any time. You have been warned!

RIGHT *Mummified corpses are well known in Ireland. Here the bodies in the vaults of St. Michan's Church in Dublin show what might be found if anyone were brave or foolish enough to open Abhartach's grave.*

The English Vampire

THE VAMPIRE OF CROGLIN GRANGE
(1873–92)

Do vampires exist in England? Perhaps the most terrifying British tale about them comes from Croglin Grange in Cumberland. It appears in a book written in 1896 by Augustus Hare, entitled The Story of My Life, as told to him by one Captain Fisher, whose family owned Croglin, and every word of it is true....

C S HARPER

LEFT *The dreadful bloodsucking fate that the Croglin Grange vampire had planned for the Cranswell's sister. Would she survive his attack?*

Croglin Grange was a very old, long, low hall in the Northwest of England, near the Scottish borders. It stood on a hill where the land sloped down to an equally ancient church. Sometime in the early 1800s, the Fisher family, who owned it, moved out and it was rented to a family called Cranswell – two brothers and a sister. They moved in during the winter and spent time getting settled and becoming part of the community.

The following summer was particularly hot – so hot that few people could sleep well in the humid nights. One night, everybody at Croglin Grange had gone to bed early, but the sister was sitting up in bed reading near the window, which had the shutters open to let in some air. She could look out across the countryside toward a dark clump of trees with the old church and its cemetery beyond.

She suddenly became aware of two lights moving from the churchyard toward the house. As they came closer, they seemed

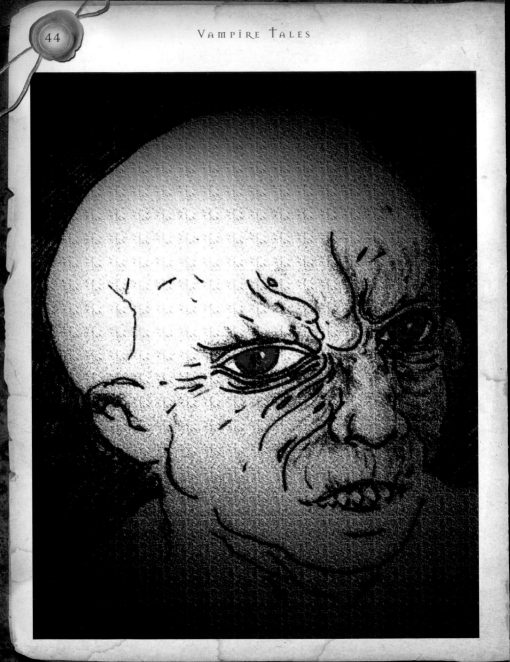

to materialize into a dark figure, traveling very fast and approaching her bedroom window in the most menacing fashion.

Leaping from her bed, the sister went to escape and as she turned, she saw that a horrible brown face, the color of withered leaves, pressing against the glass, and two red eyes, like burning coals, were now fixed directly on her. She couldn't move!

Then she heard a sound like scratching, and realized to her horror that the creature was using its long fingernails to pick the lead from around the window frame to get in. In an instant it had opened the window and was inside. Darting across the room, the ghastly creature bit the terrified young woman on the neck. The pain freed her voice and she screamed in agony and fear. Her brothers, who heard her, smashed the lock of her door and dashed into the room.

At their approach the Thing fled, and although one of the brothers chased it, it traveled in great leaping strides down toward the churchyard wall, where it disappeared into the

LEFT The terrifying face at the window. Imagine the Cranswell's sister's horror at waking to these blood-red eyes staring at her through the glass.

shadows. The sister was dreadfully hurt but no further action was taken – except that the family decided to leave Croglin Grange to vacation in Switzerland to recover.

On their return the following spring, which was as warm as the previous summer, the nights were still very clammy. One night the sister was awakened by the sound of long fingernails scratching at the glass of her bedroom window. Looking up, she saw the same horrid, ancient face with its burning eyes staring in at her.

This time her voice didn't fail her, and her screams brought her brothers immediately. They quickly chased the creature as it fled. One discharged a gun shot, which seemed to hit, but the creature vanished into the shadows at the vault of a long-extinct family.

The next morning, with the help of some neighbors, they opened the vault. It held many coffins, one of which was intact but the lid was loose. Inside lay the creature. There were even traces where the pistol shot had hit it. The body was taken out into the daylight and burned, and from then on peace reigned once again at Croglin Grange.

ROBERT THE BRUCE AND
THE SCOTTISH VAMPIRE

Certain well-known historical figures have had encounters with vampires — at least, that's what the stories tell us. One of the most famous was the celebrated Scottish king, Robert the Bruce (Robert I).

A tale concerning this monarch and the Undead was widely circulating during the fourteenth century and appears in some documents from that period.

Once, King Robert was visiting a powerful lord in Berwick, where he was well entertained with food, drink, and dancing, as was common at the time when the King visited.

During the festivities, a wild man from the forest was brought before the lord, having been accused of poaching – the penalty for which was death. This man was known locally as a fearsome thug who had caused trouble for people who lived on the lord's lands, so the lord did not hesitate to order his execution. But the King intervened, and spared his life.

However, as soon as Robert had left, the wild man was arrested once again and was executed in defiance of the Royal decree. Shortly after, a creature bearing striking resemblance to the wild man began to stalk the area, breaking into houses, attacking people in their beds, and *drinking their blood*. Disease and illness also followed the vampire and spread throughout the area.

Feeling desperate, the people called on King Robert to return and punish the local lord for disobeying him. Robert did so, instructing his soldiers to go to the executed man's grave to dig up the body, cut it into pieces, and burn it.

From that moment, the walking dead no longer troubled the people. It is said, however, that his ashes were placed in a jar and buried under a large stone near the town. If the stone is raised and the jar opened, the vampire will rise once more.

RIGHT *The brave king and vampire slayer, Robert the Bruce.*

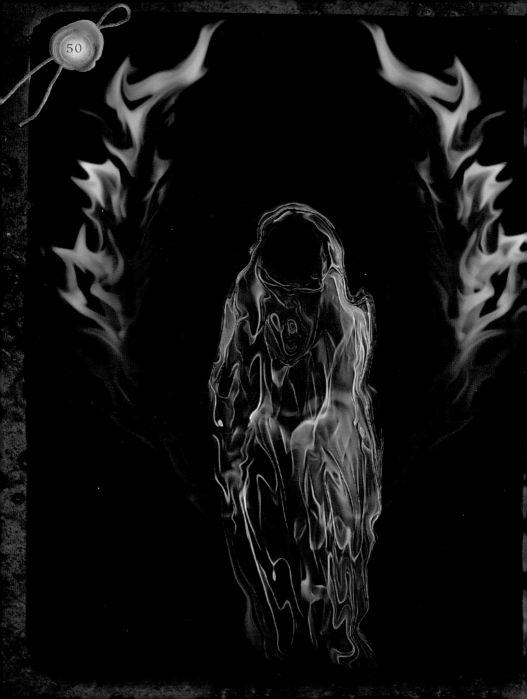

Calmet traveled to Eastern Europe, where he was appalled at the number of graves that had been dug up by vampire hunters in an attempt to find and destroy the Undead, which were said to be troubling their communities. Many corpses had been placed on fires and burned, much to the distress of their relatives, and this both shocked and saddened Calmet.

Nevertheless, he listened to the eerie stories that local people told him and wrote them all down as part of his report. And it seems that he probably believed many of them.

He recorded two of the more famous stories – that of Arnold Paole and Peter Plogojowitz, who appear later in this book, but there were others as well.

One story tells of a shoemaker in Silesia (on the border of modern-day Poland) who had taken his own life and returned from the grave to torment both his own family and the whole community.

Calmet eventually sent his report, written in French, to the Vatican. From what he had heard, he concluded that vampires were in fact the corpses of the dead. They had been brought to life by some dreadful power, and they must drink the blood of the living in order to keep themselves alive and give themselves energy.

However, Calmet also thought that these were not necessarily the bodies of evil or pagan men (those who did not believe in the Christian, Islamic, or Jewish faiths), otherwise all of early Rome, which was pagan, would have risen as vampires. Vampires, he said, might be redeemed through the love of God, because it had been God who created them, just as He had created men.

Calmet's work was seriously considered by the Vatican and was then published in a number of languages – though not in English. This was a time when many learned European men were considering what vampires might be and if they were a threat. Calmet's report gave them something to think about and discuss.

It was also the greatest collection of vampire stories written, and it continued to spook much of Europe, even long after Calmet had returned to his monastery. In many ways it was Augustin Calmet who gave us the picture of the vampire, which has continued to the present day.

LEFT *While he studied vampire stories, Dom Augustin Calmet heard tales of fiery deaths and the dead coming back to life to terrorize the living.*

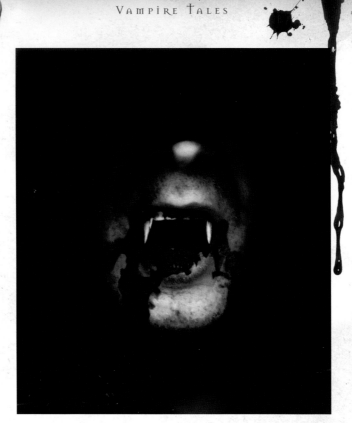

THE SOLDIER VAMPIRE
ARNOLD PAOLE

One of the instances of alleged vampirism investigated by the vampire-hunter Dom Augustin Calmet was the eerie case of Arnold Paole...

Arnold Paole was a likeable, good-natured young man who, during the mid-1700s, lived in the district of Medvegia in Serbia, which at that time was part of the Austrian Empire. Extremely good-looking, he was engaged to be married to a local girl, but before the wedding he was conscripted into the Emperor's army, fighting in Turkish Serbia. He served there several years, returning home again in 1727 to settle down as a farmer and finally get married.

However, local people noticed that he had changed. Although still pleasant, he had become brooding and fearful, ready to jump at any shadow. And he told his fiancée a strange story. When stationed in Turkish Serbia, his regiment had been subject to the nightly attacks of a vampire. Paole joined some men sent to find and destroy the creature, and it was he who had dug up the vampire from its grave. Before he could destroy it, it had attacked him in its death throes.

Since then he had felt as if a shadow followed him. Only a week after this strange confession, Paole was killed in a fall from a hay cart and was buried locally.

Some time later, a number of people complained of seeing Arnold Paole, and shortly after some of them died from an unknown disease. The "ghost" was blamed for their deaths and the word "vampire" was soon whispered in the community. They went to Paole's grave and opened it. To their horror, the body was undecayed and was oozing fresh blood from its eyes, nose, and ears.

Paole was staked with a whitethorn stake and the corpse emitted a loud groan that was heard by everyone. But the vampire did not trouble the villagers again.

LEFT *Soldiers in the Austro-Turkish War discover the wounded body of a soldier after he was attacked by a local vampire.*

The Healthy Vampire
Peter Plogojowitz

Another vampire case investigated by Dom Augustin Calmet was that of Peter Plogojowitz. There was nothing really unusual about Plogojowitz. He was simply a sixty-two-year-old farmer who owned land near the village of Kisilova in Rhum Province, Serbia, around the time that excitement was rising about the case of Arnold Paole.

Although he had always seemed in excellent health, Peter Plogojowitz suddenly and unexpectedly took ill and died. Three nights after he'd been buried, his family was awoken by strange sounds coming from the kitchen of his house. His son came down to investigate and found the likeness of his father standing there.

The apparition asked him for food and, after eating a meal, it rose and left the house, presumably going back to the grave. The next night, however, it was back demanding more food. This time the son refused, and Plogojowitz left, giving him an evil look.

The following day the son suddenly died. His death was only the first of six in the village and, before dying, it was said that many of the victims had claimed to have seen Peter Plogojowitz peering in at them through their windows,

LEFT *Peter Plogojowitz arose from his grave a full three days after being buried. A terrifying experience for his family and friends, and even more so for those the vampire tried to bite!*

although some admitted this may have been a dream. Not only that, but some reported that Plogojowitz had also tried to bite their necks.

Local magistrates, determined to put an end to the vampire hysteria in the area, contacted the Army, who sent a Commander to investigate. He ordered Plogojowitz's grave to be opened and when the body was examined, it was as good as the day he was buried, and his hair and teeth seemed to have grown. The body was staked according to local custom and then burnt on a pyre. No other similar corpses were found locally and the Commander returned to Belgrade, reporting that Plogojowitz had indeed been a vampire.

THE LADY VAMPIRES

THE VAMPIRES OF RHODE ISLAND

(1873–92)

Is there a "vampire capital" of America, and if so, where is it? New York? Los Angeles? At least that's what the vampire films tell us. But what if it were a small hamlet in rural Rhode Island? What if the smallest State in the Union had vampire tradition that went back many hundreds of years?

That would seem to indeed be the case, for down the centuries a number of "vampire ladies" have haunted the villages around South County, spreading their curse from generation to generation.

The terrible lineage starts around 1798 with Sarah Tillinghast, an odd, dreamy girl who had a habit of visiting old cemeteries where the dead from

LEFT *Vampire lady with a fascination for corpses, pictured toying with the dead and pulling the bodies from their graves.*
RIGHT *The eerie headstone on Nelly Vaughn's grave with the haunting inscription "I am waiting and watching for you."*

the American Revolutionary War were laid to rest. She died from an unknown illness but later returned as a vampire, slowly drawing the life and vitality out of her family. Her body was dug up and burned, and for a while the vampire curse halted, only to re-emerge in 1827.

This time it was Nancy Young, the daughter of a soldier. Like Sarah Tillinghast, she also sickened and died from a mysterious illness, only to return from the grave and draw the strength from other members of her family. Her coffin was also dug up and burned on a great bonfire. Again, the vampire curse seemed to have passed until 1874, when it appeared again in Juliet Rose, daughter of a prominent South County family.

Juliet also died unexpectedly from the eerie illness and was believed to return at night, drawing energy and blood from family members in the manner of the other girls. This time her heart was cut out and burned by her anguished father, thus containing the curse until 1884, when the most famous of the "vampire ladies," Mercy Brown, threatened her family (*see page 58*).

The last of the "ladies" seems to have been Nelly Vaughn in 1889, who lies in an isolated South County cemetery and whose sinister headstone seems to sum up the whole vampire mythos – *I am waiting and watching for you.*

THE SICKNESS VAMPIRE

MERCY BROWN
(1873–92)

One of the most famous "vampire ladies" of Rhode Island was Mercy Brown — famous because her story may have influenced Bram Stoker when he wrote Dracula.

In the harsh American winter of 1883, George Brown — a farmer from Exeter Village — and his family began to experience certain strange sicknesses.

In the harsh American winter of 1883, George Brown – a farmer from Exeter Village – and his family began to experience certain strange illnesses that were a little different from the colds and flu that were going around.

His wife, Mary, normally a healthy woman, suddenly came down with some form of sickness

LEFT *The crypt at Chestnut Hill cemetery where Mercy Brown's body lay for weeks while the ground was frozen and too hard to dig a grave.*

BELOW *Prayers raised to God to release the townsfolk from the ravages of disease, even without the suggestion of vampire action.*

and by the eighth of December, she was dead. The family had little time to grieve, for by the spring of 1884, George's eldest daughter, Mary Olive, had the same strange illness. By June 6, 1884, she was also dead.

Fear began to run through the family and when the only boy, Edwin, began to suffer the same symptoms in 1889, he was sent away to Colorado Springs to recover, which he did. When he was away, however, another one of his sisters, Mercy Lena, also developed the same symptoms and died. She died in 1892 and her death brought Edwin

home again – too late to see his sister alive. But, as soon as he arrived home he was visited by church elders from the Exeter and Wickford communities, who suggested to him that an ancient evil was loose.

Doctors had been baffled by the illness, but these godly men knew what it was – a vampire. This vampire drank the blood of others in Edwin's family, causing them to die. The idea preyed on Edwin's mind, so much so that when he lay down to sleep, Mercy's face peered over the edge of his bed.

"Edwin!" her voice pleaded through the nightmare. "Please feed me! I'm cold and hungry!" He couldn't rest; he had to do something about it. Mercy had been buried at the old Chestnut Hill cemetery, but when she had died the ground had been hard and frozen and her body had been left – still coffined – on a cart in a small crypt on the edge of the graveyard. The body was still accessible.

Together with a small group of men led by a local surgeon, Harold Metcalf, Edwin went up to the crypt and they opened the coffin. After long weeks of lying there, the body should have decomposed, but Mercy Brown was as fresh as the day she had been buried. In fact, she looked as if she were just asleep. Taking a knife, Metcalf cut the heart from the cadaver, and with the liver for good measure, doused it with oil and vinegar and burnt it completely. As he did so, a sound like a massive sigh passed through the crypt, startling everybody present. They then filled the coffin with a mixture of boiling water and vinegar, completely covering the corpse. Then they sealed the coffin once more, and the Brown family hoped that this was an end to the matter.

However, the eerie events proved too much for Edwin, and within months he was also dead. With his death, the curse of vampirism seems to have more or less vanished from Rhode Island – or has it?

Of course the news of these strange rituals finally found their way into certain newspapers such as the *Providence Journal*. Shortly after Bram Stoker died, his widow found cuttings from the newspaper reports on the case among some possessions he had brought back from America. So maybe Mercy Brown did in some way influence the writing of the greatest vampire story ever.

ABOVE *Mercy Brown's grave in Exeter, Rhode Island. After her death,
Mercy's grave became the center of much vampire gossip.*

The Castle Vampire

The Countess Elga

On March 10, 1909, a Viennese newspaper reported that local people living in a remote part of Eastern Europe had burned an old castle in their area and had supposedly put an end to a vampire curse.

The report may have covered a curious story that the famous writer on ghosts, the Reverend Montague Summers, linked in his book *The Vampire in Europe* to an old legend that he had heard.

A friend of his had visited a castle in a remote part of Romania and had heard a strange tale from the old couple who looked after the place. Apparently, the castle had once been owned by an old count who had one beautiful daughter named Elga. One day while riding, Elga's horse stumbled, threw her, and, tragically, she died from her injuries and was laid to rest in the castle vaults.

Soon after, the old Count himself died mysteriously, but for a while after things remained quiet. Then suddenly, local people, especially young children, began to die at an alarming rate. Some people claimed to have seen the Countess Elga walking around in the grounds of the old castle and the locals now suggested that she, and perhaps her father, had become vampires.

Elga's portrait in the great hall was said to follow visitors with its eyes and the elderly couple who looked after the castle complained of hearing noises and voices in some of

ABOVE *The castle Countess Elga stalked after her untimely death.*
LEFT *Countess Elga's vampire form would have been recognizable as the old Count's beloved daughter.*

the closed-up rooms, some of which they thought sounded just like the young Countess.

The Reverend Summers' friends claimed to have seen the Countess wandering the castle, dressed as she was in the portrait. While there was no evidence of vampire activity, visitors suddenly and inexplicably became very weak.

Was the castle the same one that the newspaper article mentioned? Summers seemed to think that it was, and that the unquiet Countess Elga might now have been laid to rest.

force of gravity drag them down, disemboweling them. This earned him the further nickname of Vlad Tepes or Vlad the Impaler.

Like his father, he was a skillful politician and made alliances with the Hungarians and sometimes even the Turks in order to protect his own interests. In 1462, Vlad was forced to flee as the Turks invaded Wallachia, and instead placed his brother, Radu the Handsome, on the throne. Vlad sought refuge in Hungary but was arrested and imprisoned by the Hungarian king Matthias on a charge of treason for his dealings with the Turks.

By 1474, however, he was free again, and with an army from Transylvania, he managed to regain his kingdom. His rule was troubled, and when the Transylvanian army left, the Turks invaded again. Vlad raised an army to fight them, but the Turkish forces were too strong and he was killed in battle near present-day Bucharest. His body was said to have been collected by monks and he was buried, as a great hero, in the island monastery at Snagov (but

this may be only a legend). Nobody knows for sure where his grave really is.

But did the Wallachian ruler actually drink blood? He was certainly very cruel and despotic in his ways, but in Eastern Europe he is usually regarded as a great leader and soldier who stood up for his people and would do anything for his country. He did many vicious things, like burning beggars, killing Saxon merchants when they came to see him, and nailing the hats of Turkish ambassadors to their heads when they refused to show him respect by taking them off, but there is no evidence that he ever drank human blood. However, over the years all sorts of legends have become attached to him – that he was a black magician, that he could change shape, and that he magically knew what was going on in the country, although this may be due to the fact that he had a great network of spies.

The story of this bloodthirsty warlord appealed to the Irish writer Bram Stoker, who wrote what is perhaps the most famous book on vampires, which he named *Dracula* in honor of this vicious man.

LEFT *The most famous vampire ever known has been played many times in movies, each role more bloodthirsty than the last.*

The Countess Dracula

Countess Elizabeth Bathory

(1873–92)

In Hungarian folklore, she is often described as "the Countess Dracula" and is known as "the woman who bathed in blood." To the rest of the world, she was the Countess Elizabeth Bathory, mistress of Csejthe Castle, a powerful Transylvanian noblewoman and widow of a great Hungarian hero.

The Bathory family was an old and illustrious one – one of the oldest in Transylvania. The line, however, was tainted by various miserable marriages, despite the fact that Elizabeth's mother, Anna, was the sister of King Stephen of Poland and her father, George, was ruler of several countries.

Elizabeth was born into the troubled family in 1560, possibly the second child of the marriage. Her

Right *The beautiful and monstrous Countess Elizabeth Bathory as a young woman.*

childhood was a difficult one and in 1571 (aged 11) she was promised in marriage to Count Francis Nadasdy (then aged 15), one of the wealthiest and most eligible bachelors in Hungary. They were married in 1575 and Elizabeth was sent to live with her mother-in-law, the formidable Lady Ursula Kasnizsai, who was widely regarded as a witch.

It was a time of plagues and
epidemics in Hungary, and tides
of disease lapped around the
walls of her castle at Savarin.
It was said that in the castle
Elizabeth was being trained
in the arts of sorcery
by the Devil, brought
there by the old Lady's
invitation. When
her mother-in-law
died, she went to
join her husband at
remote and eerie
Csejthe Castle.
Francis, however,
was a soldier
and spent most
of his time in the
Hungarian army,
leaving her alone in
the gloomy fortress.
While there, she
appears to have fallen
under the influence of
some servants – an old
maid named Darvula in
particular, a woman who
many said was a sorceress.
In 1600, Count Francis
was killed in a battle against the
Turks, making his wife mistress of
Csejthe. She was, however, growing old

and her evil life was physically catching up with her. One evening, while brushing her hair, a maid had accidentally hurt her and, taking a long, spiked brush, Elizabeth hit her, drawing blood. Later, she noticed that where the blood had fallen on her hand, the skin seemed much fresher. This set Elizabeth off on a long and murderous trail because Darvula advised her that if she were to bathe in the blood of virgins, she would regain her youth and looks.

Between 1600 and 1611, she and her servants began to murder young girls who sought employment at the castle, and the Countess drank and bathed in their blood. However, such horrors could not go undetected and local gossip soon reached the ears of King Matthias of Hungary. In 1611, the King commenced a series of trials against Elizabeth and her servants. Darvula and several of the others were found guilty and were executed, but because of her noble rank, Elizabeth was not. Matthias, however, thought she had a case to answer and commanded that she remain at Csejthe as punishment.

To this end, stonemasons were brought in and a section of the castle

BELOW *The remains of Csejthe Castle where Elizabeth, and many others, died.*

BELOW *Without the blood of young women, the Countess would have withered and aged.*

was walled up with the Countess inside. All windows were sealed and only a small hole was left where she could receive food. On July 31, 1613, Elizabeth, then aged 54, dictated her will to two Hungarian priests and shortly after she died alone in her lightless world.

By order of Matthias, her records were sealed for one hundred years, and her name was forbidden to be mentioned, as was the name "Csejthe." Even so, the shadow of Elizabeth Bathory falls across her lands – even today.

Vampire Companions

What sort of things do you associate with the vampire?
Things that might stalk you and drink your blood?

Wolves and Werewolves

In Eastern European folklore, vampires and wolves have a close relationship; in fact, a vampire can sometimes turn itself into a wolf in order to follow its prey or escape detection. It was also thought that vampires could command wolves to do their bidding and they controlled the vast packs of them that prowled through the Eastern European forests. It was also believed that if a person had been turned into a werewolf while he or she was living, they would become a vampire as soon as they died.

Spiders

Do spiders drink blood? Can there be a vampire spider? Yes, all spiders can give you a bite and some of the bigger ones can draw blood. But there *is* a spider in East Africa that depends on blood to make it appear more attractive to female spiders. Its name is *Evarcha Culicivora*, but don't worry – it will not attack humans directly. Instead, it attacks mosquitoes that have already gorged themselves on human blood. They can then emit a smell, not unlike the smell of blood, which makes them fabulously attractive to female spiders.

Above *A vampire bat swoops in for a hot and bloody meal.*
Right *The bloodsucking* Evarcha culicivora *spider, with fangs raised and ready to attack.*

Bats

Again, in some parts of the world it is believed that vampires can turn themselves into bats, sometimes to enter a house and attack those who are sleeping inside. But there *is* a vampire bat in South America (although its existence was only found long after people had been telling vampire stories for centuries). This bat *does* drink blood from sleeping humans, though it doesn't attack their neck but rather the soles of the feet. It can gently lap away the skin and draw blood without the sleeper even waking up. This leaves the sleeper exhausted and weak when he or she wakes up, just as he or she would be after a real vampire attack.

So always be careful – *the vampire is not alone!*

VAMPIRE WORLD

From Canada to Australia to China, the world is filled with vampire lore, but there are certain places that lay a terrible claim on the origins of vampire horror. Each holds true tales of the bloodthirsty Undead, but the effects of these monsters are felt worldwide.

1. New England, U.S.A.
The heartland of North American vampires.

2. Mexico
One of the main homes of the fiery Energy vampires.

3. South America
Another major source of Energy vampires.

4. Ireland
Home to the ancient tales of blood-drinking chieftans.

5. Scotland
From ancient stories to modern Strigoii tales.

6. England
Striigoi and Energy vampires plague English cemeteries.

7. Scandinavia
The land of the fearsome Draugr and their Viking treasures.

8. Poland
Silesia gave rise to the greatest vampire hunter, Dom Augustin Calmet.

9. Hungary
Elizabeth Bathory fed on blood in Hungary's Savarin province.

10. Romania
The Strigoii homeland, birthplace of Dracula and Countess Elga, the most infamous vampires of all time.

11. Greece and Crete
The land of the subtle and secretive Vrykokolas vampires.

12. Bosnian Alps, Albania
Mountain realm of the high-heeled Sampiro vampires.

13. Serbia
Home of the restless dead, Peter Plogojowitz and Arnold Paole.

14. Russia
Vampire tales abound from each corner of this vast land.

15. Israel
The Dybukk vampires hail from Israel, where they're kept at bay with charms and ribbons.

16. Ghana (Gold Coast)
Stamping ground of the Tikoloshie vampire wizards who feed on the blood of local tribes.

17. South Africa
Tikoloshie tales of those turned to vampirism by witch spells.

18. Philippines
The Aswang vampires feed nightly on blood and sweat in the Philippine Islands.

19. Malaysia
Home of the violent and terrifying Penanggal vampires.

VAMPIRE TESTS

If you are in danger of being alone with a vampire, there are various tests you can perform. If the answer to any of the questions is no, you're probably safe… maybe.

PHASE ONE

Carefully check the coloring of your vampire suspect. Does he or she have unusually pale skin? Is it almost translucent, as if it hasn't been in the sun for years?

▼ Yes

If yes, are they also elegantly thin, youthful, and yet have a worldly air about them? Do they seem knowing in ways that are not quite understandable to you?

▼ Yes

If yes, look for telltale signs of reddening in the eyes and hair. Even the most recently turned vampires will effect some outward signs of change. Keep checking.

▼ Yes

If yes, you are quite possibly in the company of a vampire.

PHASE TWO

Phase two begins with the sunlight test. Is your suspect unwilling to venture into daylight, even for the most pleasant reasons? Are they even a little scared?

▼ Yes

If yes, try to maneuver them into a strong light of some kind – even lamplight will do. Do they cast a shadow? Can you see their shape upon the wall or table?

▼ Yes

If not, it's time to push the proof. Get them in front of a mirror if possible. It's often wise to carry your own for just these occasions. Can you see their reflection in the glass?

▼ Yes

If not, it seems likely that your companion is indeed a vampire.

PHASE THREE

Phase three requires a steady nerve. Here is where you tempt your suspect into revealing his or her true nature. Start carefully. Check where your companion sleeps. Is it a coffin?

If yes, you're close but need more proof. Ask about pets. Is his or her favorite animal a bat, spider, or anything that howls at the moon?

Yes

If yes, it's pretty much time to cut to the chase. Bring up the subject of blood, perhaps in a story of having cut yourself. Is your suspect unnaturally interested?

Yes

The signs are all there; it's a good idea to be on your guard.

PHASE FOUR

The final phase is perhaps the most dangerous. By now, it's pretty clear what you're up to. Quickly whip out your trusty garlic head, or a bunch to be safe. Does your suspect recoil in horror?

Yes

If yes, bring out the silver. Is your companion now making his or her escape or becoming no more than a whisp of air?

Yes

If yes, unless you're very handy with a wooden stake, it's now abundantly clear that you have on your hands a bona fide vampire...

OK, just RUN!

GLOSSARY

Art of Sorcery
The secrets of witchcraft and wizardry, sometimes also known as the Dark Arts.

Bram Stoker
The Irish novelist who created the world's most famous vampire in his 1897 novel *Dracula*.

Church Elders
Senior members of any major Christian religion.

Coffin
Also known as a casket, a box used to hold the deceased remains for burial.

Corpse
A dead body.

Crypt
A vault or underground burial chamber, usually beneath a church.

Demon
An evil spirit. One of the servants of the Devil.

Devil
The most powerful evil spirit in the Christian faith.

Dracula
The Romanian warrior and leader who became the most famous vampire in the world.

Dragon
A legendary, winged creature that resembles a large lizard, covered with scales.

Energy
In vampire lore, this is the lifeforce of a human being that can be drained by a vampire instead of blood.

Exorcism
The removal of evil spirits from a person using the power of prayer.

Folklore
Stories and traditional tales that have been held as part of a community for generations.

Holy Water
Water that has been blessed by a priest – used in christenings and exorcisms.

Pagan
Beliefs and activities that do not belong to the major religions.

Plague
A highly infectious disease that spreads rapidly, infecting and killing many.

Sepulchre
A type of burial chamber or tomb, often carved into the rock of a hillside.

Spirit
The non-physical part of a person that is believed to exist after death. A ghost or supernatural being.

Stake
A sharpened, pointed wooden post or stick. The favored method for suspending a vampire.

Telepathy
The power to communicate mentally.

Transylvania
The Eastern European area most usually associated with vampires.

Undead, the
Beings that have become reanimated after death.

Vampire
An aggressive blood- or energy-sucking reanimated corpse. An Undead.

Winding Sheet
The cloth that a corpse is wrapped in. A burial cloth.

İΠDEX

Index continued

Acknowledgments

The publisher thanks the following agencies and illustrators for their kind permission to use their images.
b = bottom   c = center   t = top   l = left   r = right

Pages:1 Shutterstock/Tamara Kulikova/FilipFuxa/Vaclav Volrab; **2** Shutterstock/Riddle Photography/Dmitrijs Bindemanis; **4** Shutterstock/Kovacevic; **5** Corbis/Pascal Deloche/Godong; **6t** The Ronald Grant Archives/Largo Entertainment; **6b** Corbis/Bettmann Archives; **7t & 7b** Mary Evans Picture Library; **8** Corbis/Bettmann Archives; **9t** Mary Evans Picture Library; **9b** Bridgeman Art Library/Private Collection; **10** Shutterstock/ChipPix; **11t** Alamy/Tony Lilley; **11bl** Corbis/Frans Lanting; **11br** Bridgeman Art Library/Max Koepke; **13** Shutterstock/Csaba Peterdi; **14** Alamy/Joshua Abbott; **15** Lord Price Collection; **16tl** & **16tr** Mary Evans Picture Library; **17t** Shutterstock/Mike Norton; **17b** St. Augustine Museum, Florida; **18** Shutterstock/Dmitrijs Bindemanis; **21** Corbis/Bettmann; **23** Bridgeman Art Library/Victoria & Albert Museum; **24** Werner Forman Archive/Private Collection; **25** Shutterstock/Roberto Cerruti; **27** Corbis/Martin Harvey; **28-29** Shutterstock/James Steidl; **30-31** Alamy/Just Greece Photo Library/Terry Harris; **33** Shutterstock/Dmitrijs Bindemanis; **34b** Bridgeman Art Library; **35** Shutterstock/Mikhail; **36bl** Corbis/Joe McDonald; **36-37** Shutterstock/Kojot; **39** Alamy/Kim Haughton; **40-41** Corbis/Destinations; **42** Lord Price Collection; **43** Kobal Collection/Gaumont; **44** Andrew L Paciorek; **45** Shutterstock/NT Studio; **46** Corbis Premium RF/Alamy; **47** Shutterstock/Rachelle Burnside; **48** Mary Evans Picture Library; **49** Kobal Collection/Universal/Industrial Light & Magic; **50** Shutterstock/Mark Payne; **52** Shutterstock/Margaret M Stewart; **53** Mary Evans Picture Library; **54** Shutterstock/Aleks K; **55** Corbis/Daniel Smith; **56** Bridgeman Art Library; **57** J Benjamin/Flickr; **58** Joshua McGinn/Flickr; **59** Bridgeman Art Library/Private Collection/Bonhams; **61** Joshua McGinn/Flickr; **62** Kobal Collection/AIP; **63** Getty Images/Bridgeman; **64** akg-images/Schloss Ambras/Erich Lessing; **65tl** Shutterstock/NTStudio; **65tr** Shutterstock/Insuratelu Gabriela Gianina; **66** Kobal Collection/Hammer; **68-69** Topfoto; **70** Alamy/Isifa Image Service SRO/Bocik Andrej; **71** Kobal Collection/Hammer Films; **72bl** akg-images; **72cr** Shutterstock/Perov Stanislav; **73t** Corbis/Joe McDonald; **73b** Shutterstock/Fivespots; **74-75** Shutterstock/Javarman; **77** Shutterstock/Shawn Hine.